Knitting Dishcloths
Lovely Knitting Patterns for Your Home

Introduction

Looking for a simple, practical project? What about a quick and easy dishcloth? Knitted dishcloths and washcloths are the perfect instant gratification project – they're easy to make and can be finished in an afternoon.

These small hand-knit items work up quickly and give you the opportunity to practice knitting techniques that may be new to you. Plus, everyone needs at least a few on hand, making them excellent gifts for others... or yourself!

You might think that knitting dishcloths would be fairly basic, but you can find so many patterns that mix up the design and keep it interesting.

Grab a skein of your favorite cotton yarn to get started. And after you make a few, you may even look forward to a sink filled with dishes!

Supplies Needed

1. Yarn

Choosing yarn for your first project will depend on the project. So the first step should be picking a project and you can begin by answering the following questions:

- What weight of yarn do you need?
- How much yarn do you need?
- Do you need a basic yarn or a novelty yarn?
- Is there a particular fiber you want to use? You don't have to pick what was used in the pattern, but as a beginner, that is often helpful because you can easily compare your finished project to the picture in the pattern.

2. Needles

There are many, many different kinds of needles available, in a dizzying array of materials, from aluminum to rosewood, casein to bamboo.

When you're just starting out knitting, you will probably find yourself buying new needles for every project. It's the reality of this craft because you need needles in different sizes for different projects and it will take a few years to build up a great array of needles. You might pick up a pair of bamboo in US size 11 for a chunky scarf and a metal pair in US size 7 for a simple washcloth. You get to try out two materials and figure out if you prefer one needle over the other.

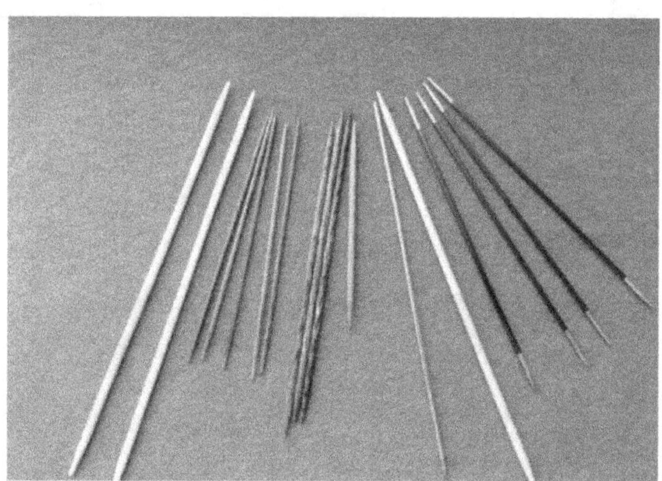

3. Other necessary Tools

- **Scissors**

In order to cut the excess yarn from your project, you need a pair of scissors.

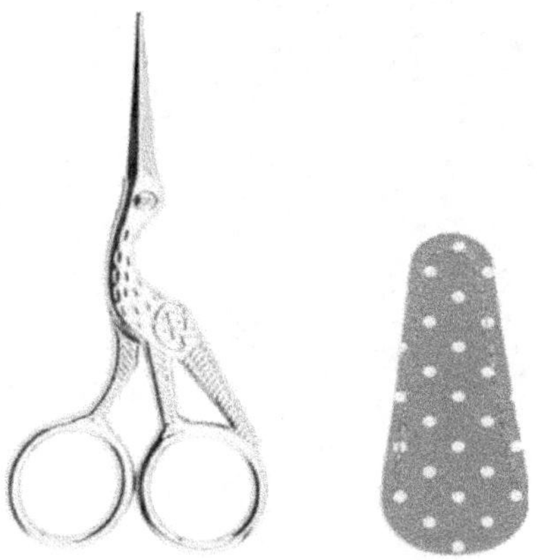

- **Sewing Needles**

Sewing needles are helpful for weaving in the ends of your knitting project and for sewing together pieces of a garment, such as putting the arms on a sweater.

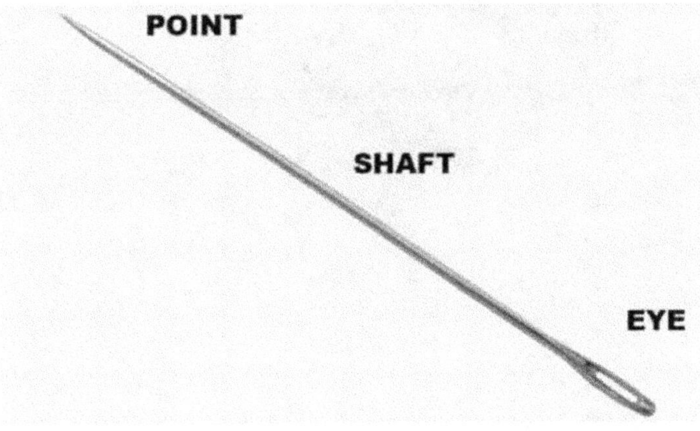

- **Stitch markers**

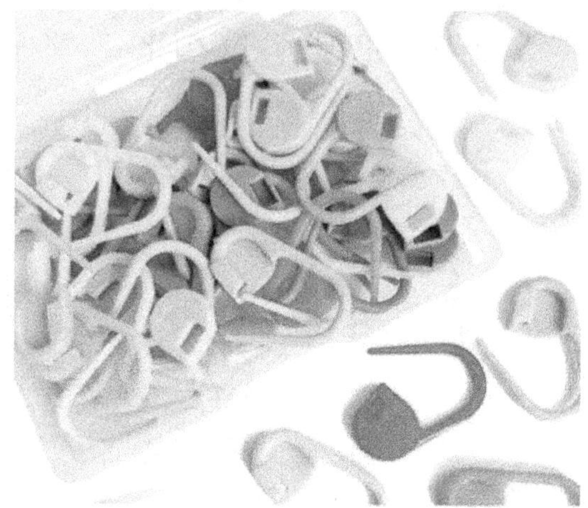

- **Measuring Tape**

Basic stitch in knitting

1. Knit

- Start by casting on however many stitches you need for your project. If you don't know how to do this, here is an easy guide to casting on your first stitches.

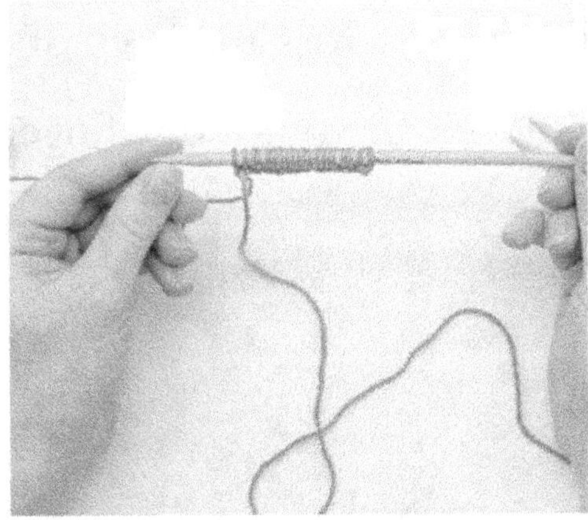

- Pick up the working needle with the cast-on stitches with your right hand. Then, wrap the working yarn around the pinky finger of your left hand clockwise two times.

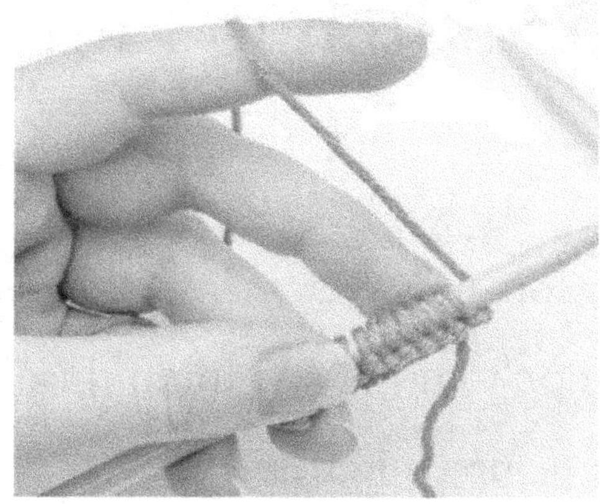

- Bring the working yarn across the back of your hands and let it rest on the last knuckle of your index finger.

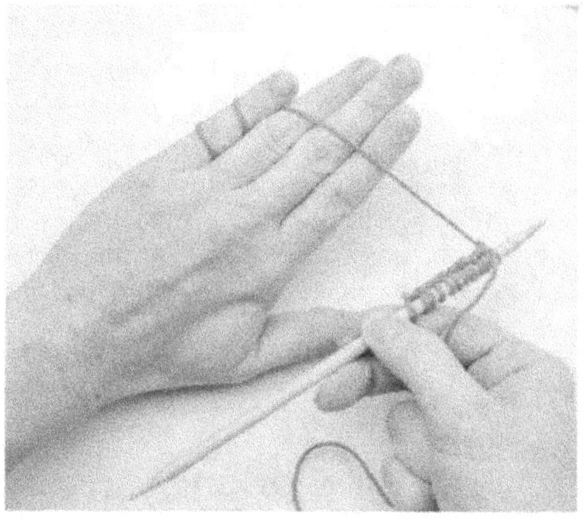

- Pick up the working needle with your left hand a bit like holding a knife, keeping your index finger almost straight. Change the angle of your index finger until there is a nice tension on the yarn. Pull the tail of the working yarn, if things are a bit too loose yet.

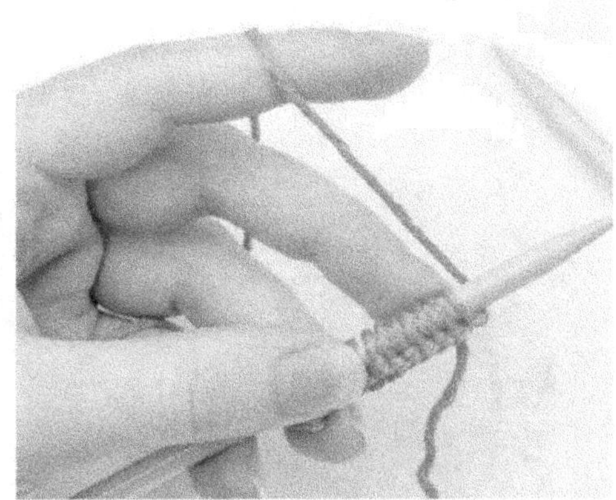

- Pick up the remaining needle with your right hand, again a bit like a knife. Keep the tension on the working yarn.

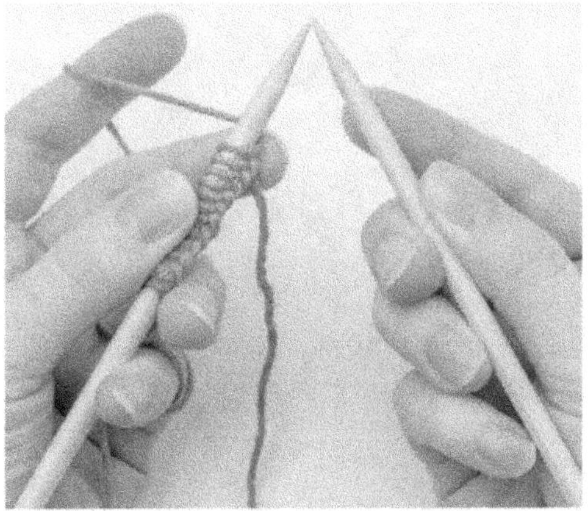

- Insert the right needle into the first loop on the left needle from the left to right. Wiggle the needle a bit around, if the loop is a bit too tight (but don't overdo).

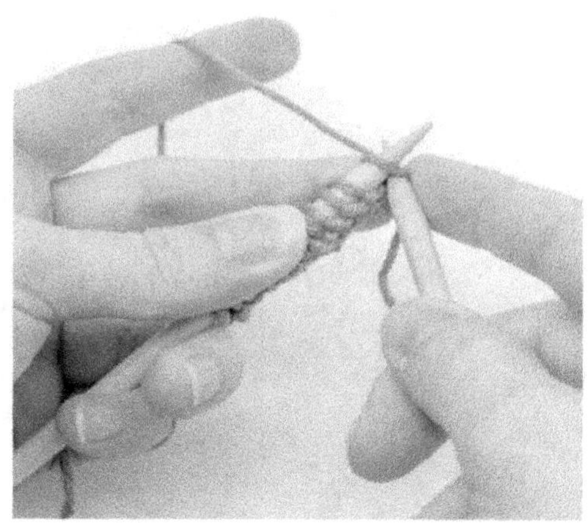

- Wrap the right needle around the working yarn (the one around your index finger) from above (counter-clockwise).

- Pull the yarn through the cast-on loop. You can use the tip of your middle finger to prevent the yarn from slipping off from the left needle as you pull it through. Don't cramp your fingers, keep a nice tension on the yarn and things will be easier.

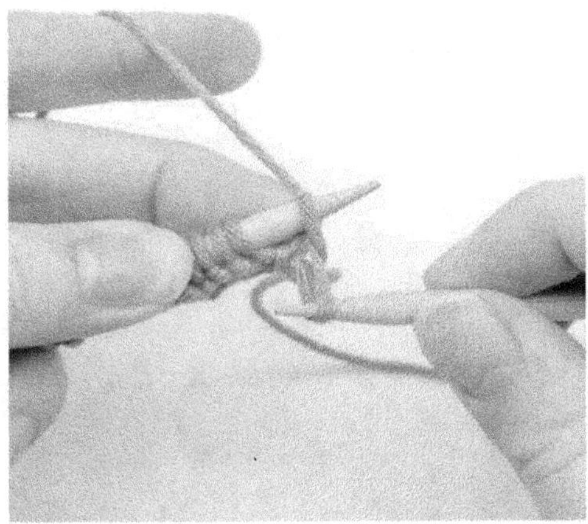

- Slip the first stitch from your left needle (I use my middle finger to push the work towards the tip and then pull the stitch off with the right needle).

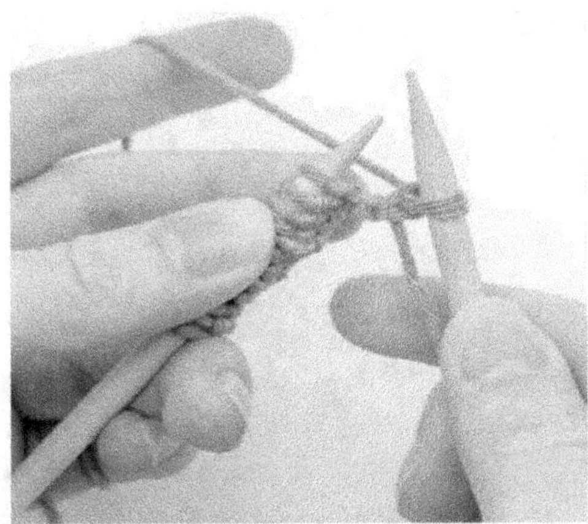

- Now, insert the right needle into the second loop from the left and repeat steps 6-9 until you are at the end of the row.

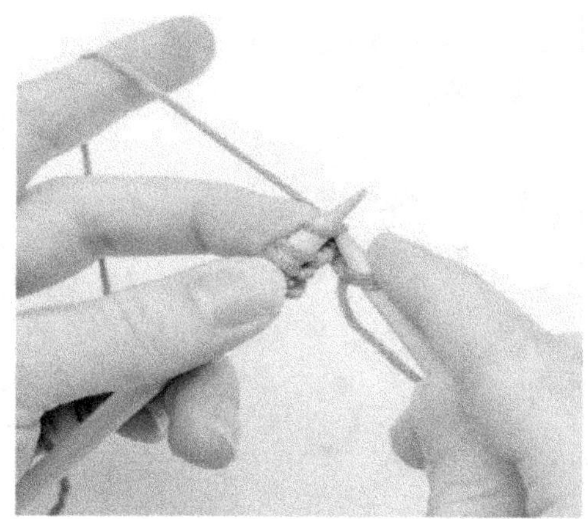

2. Purl

- Start by bringing the working yarn to the front of your work.

- Insert your right needle into the front of the first stitch on the left needle from right to left. The working yarn needs to stay in front of it all.

- Next, wrap the working yarn around the needle counter-clockwise coming from below.

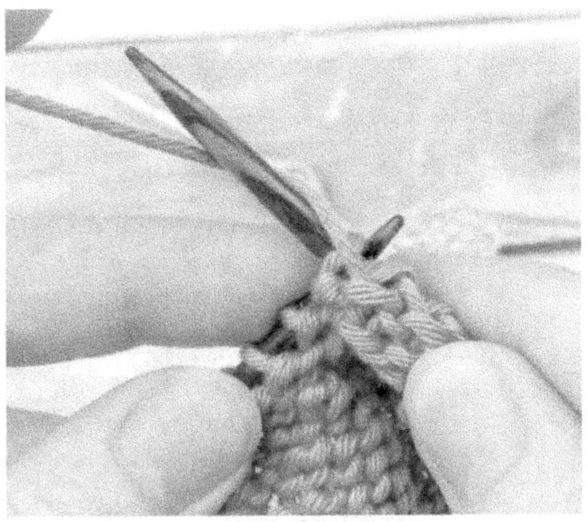

- Use your middle finger to push the working yarn forward.

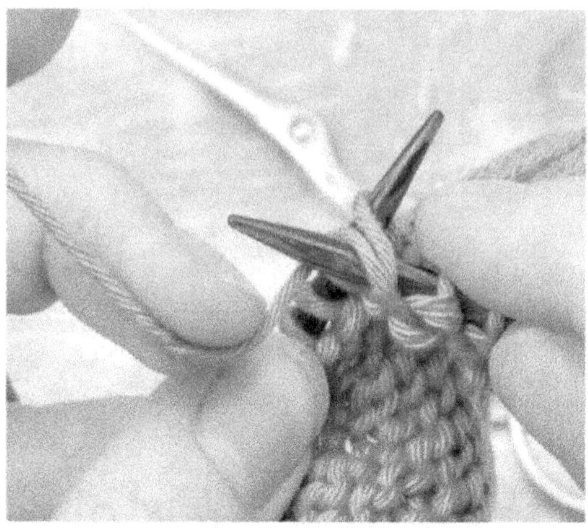

- Pull the working yarn through the stitch.

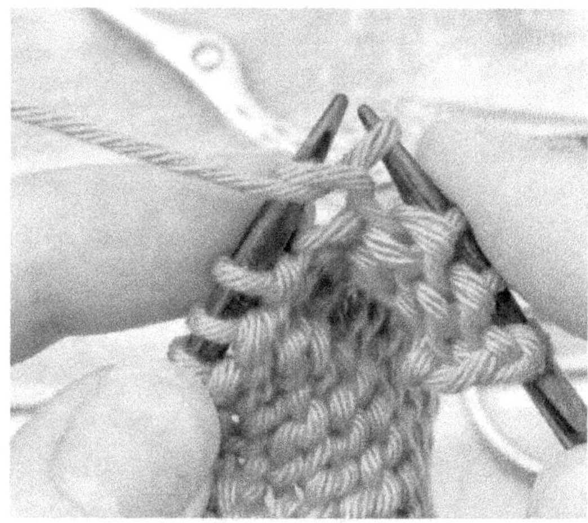

- Slip the stitch you worked through off the left needle to finish the purl stitch

3. Knit 2 together

- Start by bringing the working yarn to the back just the way you would typically for a knit stitch.

- Now, insert your right needle into the first two stitches on the left needle at the same time from left to right.

- Wrap the yarn around the needle counter-clockwise by going in from behind.

- Wrap the yarn around the needle counter-clockwise by going in from behind.

- Slip the two loops you decreased through off the left needle to finish the stitch.

4. Purl 2 together

- Bring the working yarn to the front.

- Enter the first two stitches on the left needle from right to left.

- Wrap the working yarn around the needle counter-clockwise.

- Pull the working yarn through towards the back.

- Drop both stitches off the left needle and tighten up.

5. Slip one (1)

- Bring the working yarn to the back.

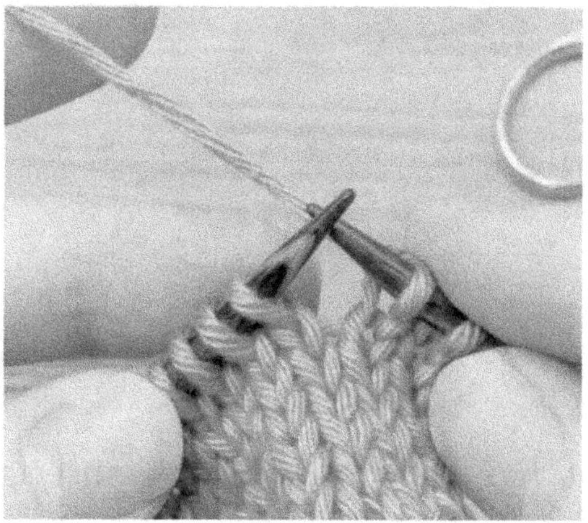

- Insert your right needle into the first stitch on the left needle from right to left (so as if to purl).

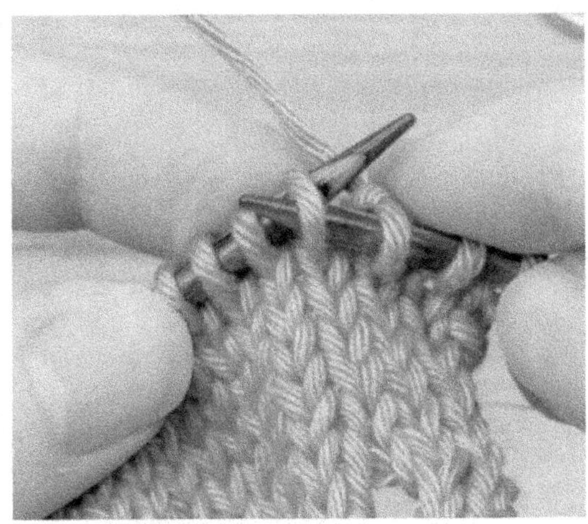

- Slip the stitch to the right needle by lifting it over (or pulling out the left needle).

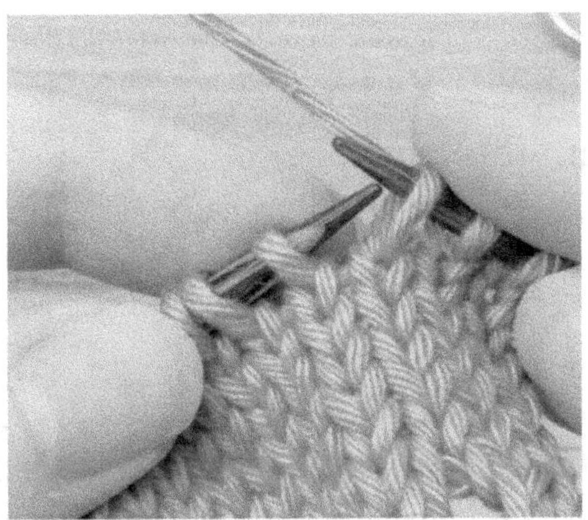

- Continue knitting as normal/according to your pattern.

6. Stockinette stitch

- Cast on any number of stitches. A moderately stretchy cast-on works best with this stitch.

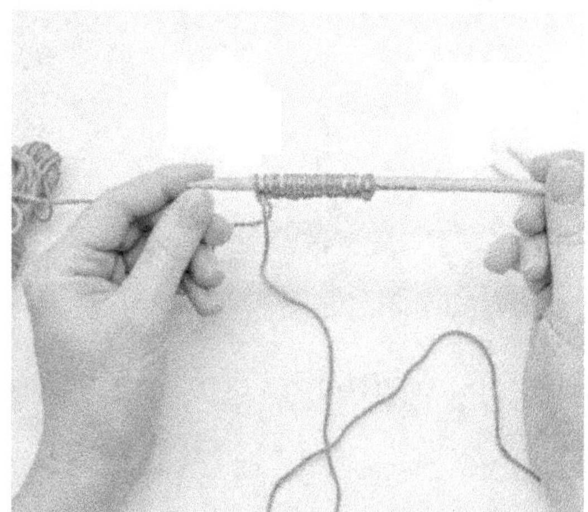

- **Row 1:** Knit across all stitches. Just the plain <u>knit stitch</u> into every loop single loop on your left needle.

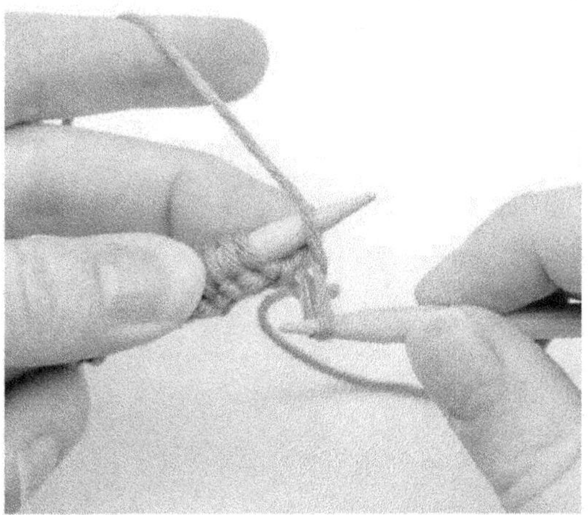

- **Row 2:** Knit purl stitches across the whole second row.

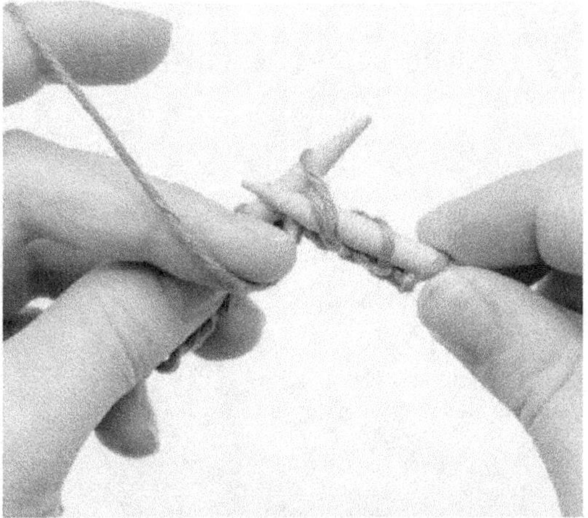

- **Repeat rows 1 and 2** until you reached the desired length. It's that easy. Just switch between knit and purl rows.

7. Slip, Slip, Knit

- Insert your right needle into the first stitch on your left needle as if to knit.

- And then simply slip that stitch onto your right needle WITHOUT knitting (you will only twist the stitch that way).

- Insert your right needle into the next stitch as if to knit, and then slip it as well.

- Re-insert your left needle into those two stitches and slip those two stitches back to the left needle again.

- And now, <u>i</u>nsert your right needle into the back loop of these two stitches

- And knit them together through back loop (k2tog tbl). And there is the finished SSK knitting stitch on your right needle. As you can see the loop leans a bit to the left.

Abbreviations

- k/ K = knit

- p/ P = purl

- k2tog/ K2TOG = knit 2 together

- p2tog/ P2TOG = purl 2 sts together

- rep/ REP = repeat(s)(ing)

- st(s)/ ST = stitch(es)

- yo/ YO = yarn over

- r/ R: Rounds

- co/ CO: cast on

- bf/ BF: bind off

- dpn/ DPN(s): double pointed needles

- pm/ PM: Place Marker

- sm/ SM: Slip Marker

- rs/ RS = Right side

- ws/ WS = Wrong side

Beautiful Patterns

1. Wash Cloths

MATRIALS

- Yarn: Fibra Natura Cottonwood (105m/50g), or any 8ply cotton, linen or bamboo yarn

- Yarn needle for sewing in ends, crochet hook in approx same size as needles (optional)

GAUGE: 20 sts x 40 rows in Garter Stitch 24 sts x 28 rows in Mosaic pattern

NOTE:

- MC Main colour

- CC Contrast colour

- M1L Make 1 left. A left leaning increase

- M1R Make 1 right. A right leaning increase

- Wyif With yarn in front

PATTERN 1 - Colourblock

This pattern has been inspired by Purl Soho's Colorblock Bias Blanket.

With MC cast on 5 sts.

Increasing

Row 1 (WS): p2, k to last 2 sts, p2.

Row 2 (RS): k2, M1L, k to last 2 sts, M1R, k2. (2 sts increased)

Repeat these two rows until you have 61 sts, or work measures approximately 20cm (or desired size).

Finish having just worked Row 2.

Decreasing

Change to CC

Row 1 (RS): k1, ssk, k to last 3 sts, k2tog, k1.

Row 2 (WS): p2, k to last 2 sts, p2.

Repeat until only 5 sts remain, and having just worked Row 1. Bind off purl-wise on WS.

Weave in ends, and attach a cord to one corner if desired. We used a 4mm crochet hook to attach the yarn and

work a crocheted chain.

PATTERN 2 – Mosaic Dots

With MC cast on 45 sts.

Knit 1 row.

Row 1: With MC, k to end.

Row 2: With MC, k to end.

Row 3: With CC, (sl1, k1) repeat to last st, sl1.

Row 4: With CC, (sl1 wyif, k1) repeat to last st, sl1 wyif.

Repeat these 4 rows until 20cm or until square.

Knit 1 row with MC, then bind off.

Weave in ends, and attach a cord to one corner if desired. We used a

4mm crochet hook to attach the yarn and

work a crocheted chain.

2. Basic Grey

MATERIALS

- 1 Skein of worsted Weight Cotton Yarn (200 yards or less)

- US size 7 (4.5 mm) 16" circular knitting needle

- A darning needle for weaving in ends

GAUGE

6 stitches equal 1 inch when using worsted weight yarn, while working in pattern. I achieve this gauge with size 7 needles, but knit your

own swatch to ensure proper cloth size!

DIRECTIONS

With your US size 7 (4.5 mm) knitting needle, CO 45 STS using your favorite cast on method.

Row 1 (WS): (K1, S1F) until 1 stitch remains, K1, turn work.

Row 2 (RS): Knit across, turn work.

Repeat these two rows a total of 30 times.

Bind off loosely.

Weave in all ends and block. Enjoy!!

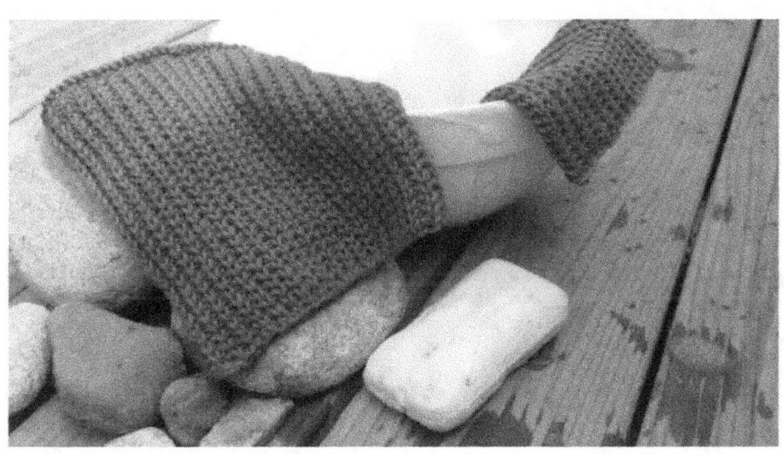

3. Practical Little Heart
MATERIALS

- Approximately 65 m (70 yards) of cotton, hemp, or linen DK or Sport weight yarn. Sample is knit in - Bernat Handicrafter Cotton; 100% cotton; 524 m/340 g; colour "salt and pepper". (If using Sport weight yarn, you may wish to knit at a slightly tighter gauge, which will result in a slightly smaller finished size.)

- Circular needle or straight needles, of a size to obtain gauge. Sample was knit on 3.5 mm / US 4 needles

- 1 stitch marker

- 1 removable marker

- 1 large stitch holder

GAUGE: Approximately 20 sts and 40 rows per 10 cm (4 inches) in garter st

NOTES

- Heart is knit from the bottom point up. Once the center diamond is complete, a semi circle is worked on each side of the top to complete the shape.

- Any time the instructions indicate "slip 1", slip the st as if to purl, with yarn held in front. This will ensure a neat edge!

- dec'd = decreased

- inc'd = increased

- kfb = knit into the front, then knit into the back of the same st

- LH = left hand

- ppso = pass previous st over

- psso = pass slipped st over

- RH = right hand

-

INSTRUCTIONS

BOTTOM OF HEART

Backward loop CO 2 sts.

Row 1 (RS): kfb, place marker, kfb. *(= 4 sts)*

Row 2 (WS): slip 1, k1, slip marker, k2.

Row 3 (RS): slip 1, kfb, slip marker, kfb, k1. *(= 6 sts)*

TIP: Place removable marker on RS of work to help keep track of which row you're working on.

Row 4 (WS): slip 1, k2, slip marker, k3.

Row 5 (RS): slip 1, k to 1 st before marker, kfb, slip marker, kfb, k to end. *(= 8 sts)*

Row 6 (WS): slip 1, k to marker, slip marker, k to end.

Repeat last 2 rows 26 more times. *(= 60 sts total; 30 sts on each side of marker)*

TOP RIGHT SEMI CIRCLE

Row 59 (RS): slip 1, k29. Remove marker. Move sts from LH needle onto stitch holder. Turn work to WS.

Row 60 (WS): slip 1, k29. Turn work.

Next 6 rows: slip 1, k to end.

Row 67 (RS): slip 1, k2 tog, k to last 3 sts, ssk, k1. *(= 2 sts dec'd; = 28 sts)*

Rows 68-72: slip 1, k to end.

Row 73 (RS): slip 1, k2 tog, k to last 3 sts, ssk, k1. *(= 2 sts dec'd; = 26 sts)*

Rows 74 - 76: slip 1, k to end.

Row 77 (RS): slip 1, k2 tog, k to last 3 sts, ssk, k1. *(= 2 sts dec'd)*

Row 78 (WS): slip 1, k to end.

Repeat previous 2 rows 3 more times. *(= 18 sts)*

Row 85 (RS): slip 1, k2 tog, k to last 3 sts, ssk, k1. *(= 2 sts dec'd)*

Repeat previous row 3 more times. *(= 10 sts)*

Row 89 (RS): slip 1, ssk, psso, *k1, ppso; repeat from * 4 more times

(2 sts remain on LH needle), k2 tog, ppso.

Cut yarn and pull through last st.

TOP LEFT SEMI CIRCLE

Move sts from holder onto LH needle.

With RS facing, join new yarn at middle of heart.

Next row (RS): slip 1, k29. Turn work to WS.

Work Rows 60 - 89 as for Top Right Semi Circle.

FINISHING

Weave in ends. Wash and dry according to yarn label. Enjoy!

4. Easy Nine Patch

MATERIALS

- Size 7 (4.5 mm) knitting needles

- 30 yards of worsted weight cotton yarn

GAUGE: 16 sts & 24 rows = 4"

INSTRUCTIONS

CO 24 sts. A long tail cast on works fine.

Rows 1-6: Knit 6 rows.

Row 7: K9, p6, k9.

Row 8: K3, p6, k6, p6, k3.

Rows 9-14: Repeat Rows 7 & 8 (3x).

Row 15: K3, p6, k6, p6, k3.

Row 16: k9, p6, k9.

Rows 17-24: Repeat Rows 15 & 16 (4x).

Row 25: K9, p6, k9.

Row 26: K3, p6, k6, p6, k3.

Rows 27-32: Repeat Rows 25 & 26 (3x).

Row 33: K9, p6, k9.

Rows 34-38: Knit 5 rows.

BO all sts. Cut yarn. Weave in all ends.

5. Eloomanator's Diagonal Knit Dishcloth

MATERIALS

- Solid color

- Worsted weight cotton or linen S

- Size 6 knitting needles

GAUGE: 4.5 sts per inch in stockinette stitch.

TIP: for cloth to lay flat, be careful to not tug on first stitch of each row.

NOTE: SKP=Slip, Knit, Pass. Slip one stitch as if to knit; knit the next stitch; pass the slipped stitch over the knitted stitch.

INSTRUCTIONS

Cast on 4 sts.

Row 1: knit

Row 2: k2, yo, knit to end.

Repeat Row 2 until there are 23 sts on needle.

Row 3: k2, yo, k9 (12 sts on right needle), yo, SKP, k remaining 10 sts.

Row 4: k2, yo, knit to end.

Row 5: k2, yo, k9, *yo, SKP. Repeat *, knit remaining 10 sts.

Row 6: as Row 4.

Repeat Rows 5 and 6, adding an additional *yo, SKP for each repeat, until there are 55 sts (or until size desired and ending with an odd number of sts).

Row 7: k1, k2tog, yo, k2tog, k8 (12 sts on right needle), *yo, SKP. Rep * until 12 sts remain on left hand needle. Knit to end.

Row 8: k1, k2tog, yo, k2tog, knit to end.

Repeat Rows 7 & 8 until interior square is eliminated.

Repeat Row 8 until 5 sts remain.

Next row: k1, k2tog, k2.

Bind off.

Variations of this pattern may be knitted by substituting K2togTBL (knit 2 together through the back loop) or SSK (slip, slip, knit) for SKP in the previous instructions). (K2tog did not work as well for me, due to gauge issues. It may work fine for you.)

6. Spa Day Facecloth
MATERIALS

- Yarn: 120 yards DK weight cotton yarn – the better quality yarn you use, the more luxurious your facecloth will feel.

- Needles: US size 6 needles

- Misc: 2 stitch markers

- tapestry needle

DIRECTIONS

Cast on 53 stitches.

Work 3 rows in seed stitch.

Row 1 (RS): Work first 3 stitches in seed stitch, place marker (pm), k to last 3 stitches, pm, work last 3 stitches in seed stitch.

Row 2: Work first 3 stitches in seed stitch, slip marker (sm), p to last 3 stitches, sm, seed stitch.

Row 3: Work first 3 stitches in seed stitch, sm, p2, k1 to last 5 stitches, p2, sm, work last 3 stitches in seed stitch.

Row 4: Work first 3 stitches in seed stitch, sm, k2, p1 to last 5 stitches, k2, sm, work last 3 stitches in seed stitch.

Repeat rows 1-4 17 times.

Repeat rows 1 & 2.

Work 3 rows in seed stitch.

Bind off loosely in pattern. Weave in ends.

(If you want to use worsted weight yarn for this pattern, use size 7 needles, cast on 44 stitches, and knit 14 repeats.)

7. Kitty Prints Dishcloth

MATERIALS

- 3.5 mm knitting needles

- 100% cotton worsted weight yarn

INSTRUCTIONS

Cast on 41 stitches

Rows 1 – 4: K (border)

Row 5 (RS): K

All even numbered rows 6 – 66: K3, P35, K3

Row 7: K

Row 9: K

Row 11: K22, P3, K1, P3, K12

Row 13: K21, P9, K11

Row 15: K21, P9, K11

Row 17: K19, P2, K1, P7, K1, P2, K9

Row 19: K18, P4, K2, P3, K2, P4, K8

Row 21: K18, P4, K7, P4, K8

Row 23: K19, P2, K9, P2, K9

Row 25: K22, P2, K3, P2, K12

Row 27: K21, P4, K1, P4, K11

Row 29: K21, P4, K1, P4, K11

Row 31: K22, P2, K3, P2, K12

Rows 33 – 41: K (odd numbered rows only)

Row 43: K12, P3, K1, P3, K22

Row 45: K11, P9, K21

Row 47: K11, P9, K21

Row 49: K8, P2, K2, P7, K2, P2, K18

Row 51: K7, P4, K3, P3, K3, P4, K17

Row 53: K7, P4, K9, P4, K17

Row 55: K8, P2, K2, P2, K3, P2, K2, P2, K18

Row 57: K11, P4, K1, P4, K21

Row 59: K11, P4, K1, P4, K21

Row 61: K12, P2, K3, P2, K22

Row 63: K

Row 65: K

Rows 67 – 70: K (Border)

Cast off.

8. Tulip Flower Dishcloth

MATERIALS

- With DK/Light Worsted Weight yarn and 4 mm (US 6, UK 8) knitting needles (highly recommend Cascade Yarns 220 Superwash Yarn.)

- With Worsted Weight yarn and and 4.5 mm knitting needles (US size 7, UK size 7) (highly recommend Cascade 220 (Aran))

- Any sized needle and yarn can be used

CHART INSTRUCTIONS

On Right Side: Knit white squares and purl black dots

On Wrong Side: Purl white squares and knit black dots

Cast on 45 stitches and start at bottom left hand corner of chart with a wrong side row.

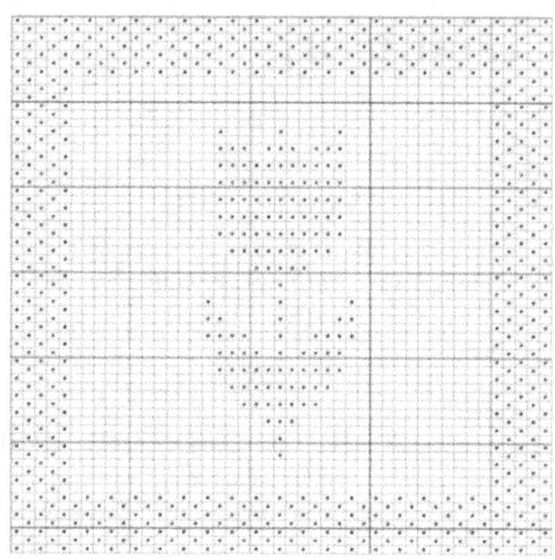

WRITTEN INSTRUCTIONS

Cast on 45

Work 7 rows of (K1,P1) to last stitch, K1

Row 8: K1, P1, K1, P1, K37, P1, K1, P1, K1

Row 9 and All Odd Numbered Rows: K1, P1, K1, P1, K1, P35, K1, P1, K1, P1, K1.

Row 10: K1, P1, K1, P1, K37, P1, K1, P1, K1

Row 12: K1, P1, K1, P1, K18, P1, K18, P1, K1, P1, K1

Row 14: K1, P1, K1, P1, K18, P1, K18, P1, K1, P1, K1

Row 16: K1, P1, K1, P1, K17, P3, K17, P1, K1, P1, K1

Row 18: K1, P1, K1, P1, K15, P7, K15, P1, K1, P1, K1

Row 20: K1, P1, K1, P1, K14, P9, K14, P1, K1, P1, K1

Row 22: K1, P1, K1, P1, K13, P11, K13, P1, K1, P1, K1

Row 24: K1, P1, K1, P1, K13, P4, K1, P1, K1, P4, K13, P1, K1, P1, K1

Row 26: K1, P1, K1, P1, K12, P4, K2, P1, K2, P4, K12, P1, K1, P1, K1

Row 28: K1, P1, K1, P1, K12, P2, K4, P1, K4, P2, K12, P1, K1, P1, K1

Row 30: K1, P1, K1, P1, K12, P1, K5, P1, K5, P1, K12, P1, K1, P1, K1

Row 32: K1, P1, K1, P1, K18, P1, K18, P1, K1, P1, K1

Row 34: K1, P1, K1, P1, K16, P5, K16, P1, K1, P1, K1

Row 36: K1, P1, K1, P1, K14, P9, K14, P1, K1, P1, K1

Row 38: K1, P1, K1, P1, K13, P11, K13, P1, K1, P1, K1

Row 40: K1, P1, K1, P1, K13, P11, K13, P1, K1, P1, K1

Row 42: K1, P1, K1, P1, K13, P11, K13, P1, K1, P1, K1

Row 44: K1, P1, K1, P1, K13, P11, K13, P1, K1, P1, K1

Row 46: K1, P1, K1, P1, K13, P11, K13, P1, K1, P1, K1

Row 48: K1, P1, K1, P1, K13, P3, K1, P3, K1, P3, K13, P1, K1, P1, K1

Row 50: K1, P1, K1, P1, K13, P1, K4, P1, K4, P1, K13, P1, K1, P1, K1

Row 52: K1, P1, K1, P1, K37, P1, K1, P1, K1

Row 54: K1, P1, K1, P1, K37, P1, K1, P1, K1

Row 56: K1, P1, K1, P1, K37, P1, K1, P1, K1

Rows 57-63: Work 7 rows of (K1, P1) to last stitch, K1

Cast off, weave in ends and block.

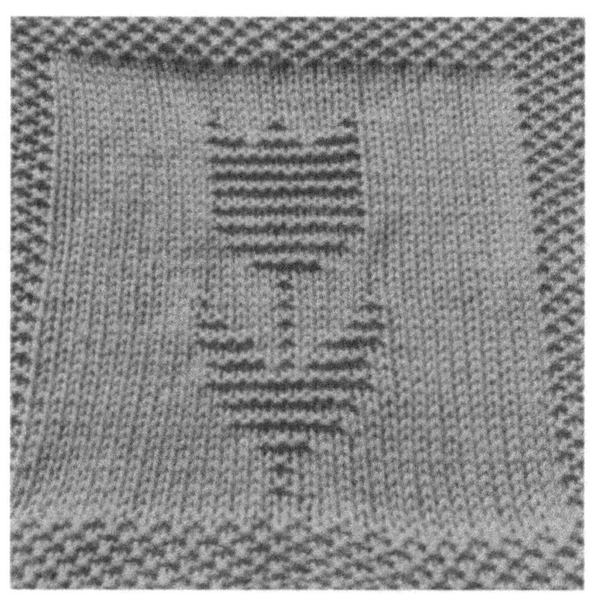

9. Leafy Washcloth

MATERIALS

- 30 yards cotton or cotton blend yarn, in DK, worsted or aran
  weight.

- 4.0 - 5.0 mm needles, depending on which yarn you use. (Check the yarn label for guidance).

- tapestry needle, 2 stitch markers

GAUGE 24 (DK), 22 (Worsted), 20 (Aran) sts = 4 inches of garter stitch. Correct gauge is not essential for this project.

PATTERN

These will be concave as you knit them, but when you wet-block them, they will take on their leaf shape.

Version 1: Garter Stitch Leaf

Cast on 3 sts.

Row 1: K1, pm, k1, pm, k1.

Row 2 (and all even rows): Knit.

Row 3: K1, m1, sm, k1, sm, m1, k1—5 sts.

Row 5: K1, m1, knit to marker, m1, sm, k1, sm, m1, knit to last st, m1, k1—9 sts.

Row 7: Rep row 5—13 sts.

Row 9: Knit to marker, m1, sm, k1, sm, m1, knit to end—15 sts. Rep rows 8-9 eight times—31 sts.

Next 9 rows: Knit.

Next row: Knit to 2 sts bef marker, k2tog, sm, k1, sm, ssk, knit to end—29 sts.

Rep the last 2 rows until there are 5 sts left on the needle.

Next row: Knit.

Next row: K2tog, remove marker, k1, remove marker, ssk—3 sts.

Next row: Knit.

Next row: K2tog, k1—2 sts.

Bind off.

Version 2: Stocking Stitch Leaf with Stem

Cast on 3 sts.

Rows 1-4: Knit.

Row 5 (RS): K1, pm, k1, pm, k1.

Rows 6 and 8: Knit.

Row 7: Knit to marker, m1, sm, k1, sm, m1, knit to end—5 sts.

Row 9: Rep row 7—7 sts.

Row 10: K3, p1, K3.

Row 11: Rep row 7- 9sts.

Row 12: K3, purl to marker, sm, p1, sm, purl to last 3 sts, k3.

Rep rows 11-12 11 times—31 sts.

Next row (RS): Knit.

Next row: Rep row 12.

Rep these 2 rows 3 times.

Next row: Knit to 2 bef marker, k2tog, sm, k1, sm, ssk, knit to end—29 sts.

Next row: Rep row 12.

Rep these 2 rows until 7 sts rem on needle.

Next row: K1, k2tog, remove marker, k1, remove marker, ssk, k1—5 sts.

Next row: Knit.

Next row: K2tog, k1, ssk—3 sts.

Next row: Knit.

Next row: K2tog, k1—2 sts.

Bind off.

FINISHING

Wet the cloth thoroughly. Lay flat, shaping into leaf, let dry. Weave in ends.

10. Farmhouse Dishtowels

MATERIALS

- Main Color: 1 skein of Purl Soho's Cotton Pure, 100% organically grown cotton. Each skein is 279 yards/ 100 grams; approximately 279 yards required.

- Contrast Color: 1 skein of Purl Soho's Cotton Pure; approximately 22 yards required.

- US 4 (3.5 mm) 24-inch circular needles

NOTES

- MIX COLORS

  MC: HEIRLOOM WHITE + CC: TOMATO ORANGE

  MC: HEIRLOOM WHITE + CC: LINDEN GREEN

  MC: HEIRLOOM WHITE + CC: CRYSTAL BLUE

- SLIP STITCHES: Slip all slipped stitches purlwise, unless the pattern indicates otherwise.

- STITCH MULTIPLE: This pattern works over a multiple of 4 + 1 stitches.

- TURN + SLIDE: When you work this Stitch Pattern, you either "turn" or "slide" the work at the end of each row.

- "Turn work" means to do what you would normally do when knitting rows with circular needles: Transfer the needle from your left hand into your right hand and the needle from your right hand into your left, flipping the work around so the opposite side is facing you.

- "Slide work" means to keep the same side of the work facing you and to push all the stitches to the right end of the circular needles. Without turning the work, start the new row as you normally would.

- You will know that you're doing this right if the yarn you need to complete the next row is right there waiting for you!

GAUGE: 31 stitches and 44 rows = 4 inches in stitch pattern

ONE-COLOR STITCH PATTERN

Row 1 (WS): With Main Color (MC), slip 1 knitwise with yarn in front (wyif), *k1, slip 1 wyif, k2, repeat from * to end of row.

Row 2 (RS): With MC, slip 1 knitwise wyif, *k3, slip 1 wyif, repeat from * to last 4 stitches, k4.

TWO-COLOR STITCH PATTERN

Row 1 (WS): With Contrast Color (CC), slip 1 wyif, *k1, slip 1 wyif, k2, repeat from * to last 4 stitches, [k1, slip 1 wyif] twice. Slide work.

Row 2 (WS): With Main Color (MC), slip 1 knitwise wyif, *p3, slip 1 with yarn in back (wyib), repeat from * to last 4 stitches, p3, k1. Turn work.

Row 3 (RS): With CC, slip 1 wyib, *p1, slip 1 wyib, p2, repeat from * to last 4 stitches, [p1, slip 1 wyib] twice. Slide work.

Row 4 (RS): With MC, slip 1 knitwise wyif, *k3, slip 1 wyif, repeat from * to last 4 stitches, k4. Turn work.

PATTERN

With Main Color (MC), use a Basic Long Tail Cast-On to cast on 85 stitches.

With MC, work One-Color Stitch Pattern (see Notes) until piece measures 1 inch from cast-on edge (repeat Rows 1 and 2 six times), ending with Row 2.

Work Two-Color Stitch Pattern (see Notes) for 1 inch [repeat Rows 1-4 three times], ending with Row 4.

Do not cut CC. Instead, can it carry up the selvage to the next time you need it.

With MC, work One-Color Stitch Pattern for 1/3 inch [repeat Rows 1 and 2 twice], ending with Row 2.

Work Two-Color Stitch Pattern for 1/3 inch [repeat Rows 1-4 once], ending with Row 4.

Cut CC.

With MC, work One-Color Stitch Pattern for 13 inches, ending with Row 2.

Work Two-Color Stitch Pattern for 5/8 inch [repeat Rows 1-4 twice], ending with Row 4.

Cut CC.

With MC, work One-Color Stitch Pattern for almost 1 inch (repeat Rows 1 and 2 five and a half times), ending with Row 1.

Bind Off (right side): K1, *[k1, slip first stitch over] 3 times, p1, slip first stitch over, repeat from * to last 4 stitches, [k1, slip first stitch over] twice, k2, leaving 3 stitches on right needle.

MAKE I-CORD

With the remaining 3 stitches, work an I-cord for 3 inches, working the last row as follows…

Last Row: K1, k2tog, pass first stitch over second stitch and off the right needle. Cut yarn, leaving an 8-inch tail and pull through remaining stitch.

Thread the tail onto a tapestry needle. Make a loop with the I-cord and weave the tail into the fabric of the Dishtowel at the base of the I-cord, then weave it through the looped I-cord, and back into the fabric of the Dishtowel.

Weave in the remaining ends and block as desired.

11. Waffle Stitch Washcloth

MATERIALS

- 1 skein of Purl Soho's Field Linen, 100% linen. Each skein is 295 yards; approximately 73 yards required for each washcloth. (Note that you use the entire skein to make all four washcloths, so to get four, please make sure your gauge is correct!)

- US 4 (3.5 mm), straight or 16-inch circular needles

- If using straight needles: Two US 4 double pointed needles for I-Cord

GAUGE: 26 stitches and 52 rows = 4 inches in stitch pattern, blocked

SIZE

NOTES

- **STITCH MULTIPLE**: This pattern works over an odd number of stitches.
- **SLIP STITCHES:** Slip all slipped stitches purlwise.

PATTERN

Cast on 43 stitches. We used a basic Long Tail Cast On.

Row 1 (WS): K1, purl to last stitch, k1.

Row 2 (RS): Knit to end of row.

Row 3: *K1, slip 1 with yarn in front (wyif, see Notes), repeat from * to last stitch, k1.

Row 4: *K1, slip 1 with yarn in back (wyib), repeat from * to last stitch, k1.

Repeat Rows 1-4 until piece measures 9 inches from cast-on edge, ending with Row 3.

With right side facing you, bind off in 1×1 rib stitch pattern. Here's how…

Bind Off Row (RS): K1, *k1, pass first stitch over, p1, pass first stitch over, repeat from * to last 2 stitches, k2, leaving 3 stitches on right needle.

MAKE I-CORD

With the remaining 3 stitches, work an I-Cord for 3 inches, working the last row as follows…

Last Row: K1, knit 2 together, pass first stitch over second stitch and off the right needle. Cut yarn, leaving an 8-inch tail. Pull through remaining stitch.

Thread the tail onto a tapestry needle. Make a loop with the I-cord and weave the tail into the fabric of the washcloth at the base of the I-cord, then weave it through the looped I-cord, and back into the fabric of the washcloth.

Weave in the remaining ends and block as desired.

12. Colorful Half + Half Washcloths
MATERIALS

- 8 skeins of Purl Soho's Cotton Pure, 100% organically grown cotton. Each skein is 279 yards/ 100 grams.

    - Color A: 4 skeins in Heirloom White; approximately 1,006 yards required for all 8 washcloths.

    - Color B: 1 skein in Jonquil Yellow; approximately 210 yards required for all 8 washcloths.

- Color C: 1 skein in Peach Peony; approximately 150 yards required for all 8 washcloths.

  - Color D: 1 skein in Tomato Orange; approximately 180 yards required for all 8 washcloths.

  - Color E: 1 skein in Moonflower Blue; approximately 230 yards required for all 8 washcloths.

- US 3 (3.25 mm) straight or 16-inch circular needles

- If using straight needles: Two US 3 double pointed needles for I-Cord

- A stitch marker

GAUGE: 24 stitches and 50 rows = 4 inches in garter stitch

NOTES

- Each washcloth requires a total of 222 yards.

- SHORT ROW SHAPING: WRP-T (WRAP AND TURN)

Keeping yarn in back, slip next stitch purlwise from left needle to right needle. Bring yarn to front. Return slipped stitch to left needle. Turn work so wrong side is facing you.

- KNIT WITH WRAP

Keeping yarn in back, pick up the wrap with the right needle from front to back, then insert the needle into the wrapped stitch knitwise. Knit the stitch and wrap together.

- CONSTRUCTION

Due to their construction, the dimensions of these washcloths are fixed to a set ratio. The width (i.e. the cast-on edge) can be altered by casting on any number of stitches, and the length will always be approximately 95% of the width.

SCHEMATIC

This is a basic schematic for the construction of the Half + Half Pattern.

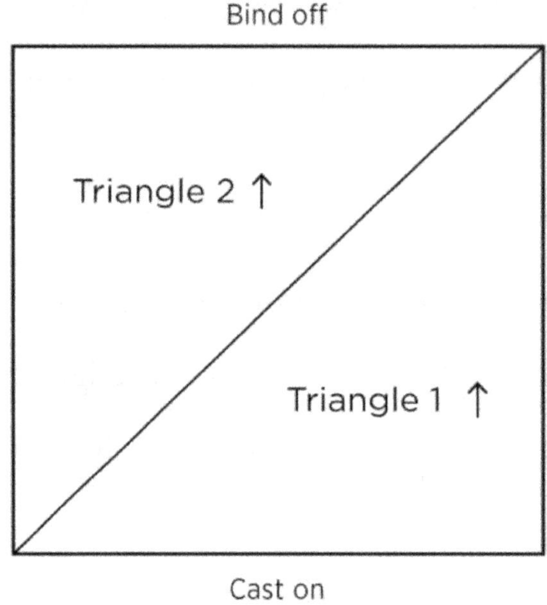

PATTERN

HALF + HALF PATTERN

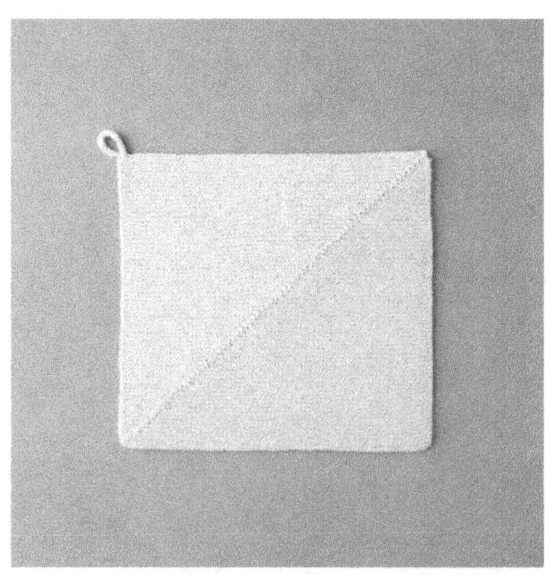

NOTE This is the foundation pattern for all the washcloths. Later we'll detail how to add stripes and colorblocks, but this simple Half + Half Pattern makes a great washcloth, too!

TRIANGLE 1

With Color B, cast on 72 stitches. We used a basic Long Tail Cast On.

Row 1 (WS): Knit to end of row.

Row 2 (RS): Knit to last 3 stitches, place marker (pm), k1, wrap and turn (wrp-t, see Notes).

Row 3: Knit to end of row.

Row 4: Knit to marker, remove marker, wrp-t.

Row 5: K1, pm, knit to end of row.

Repeat Rows 4 and 5 until you have wrapped every stitch except the last two, ending with Row 5.

Next Row (RS): K1, remove marker, wrp-t.

Next Row (WS): K1.

Cut Color B.

TRIANGLE 2

Row 1 (RS): With Color A, k1, *knit next stitch with its wrap (see Notes), repeat from * to last stitch, k1.

Row 2 (WS): Knit to end of row.

Row 3: Knit to end of row.

Row 4: K1, wrp-t.

Row 5: K1.

Row 6: K1, knit next stitch with its wrap, place marker, wrp-t.

Row 7: Slip marker, knit to end of row.

Row 8: Knit to marker, remove marker, knit next stitch with its wrap, place marker, wrp-t.

Repeat Rows 7 and 8 until you have completed a wrap and turn on the second to last stitch, ending with Row 7.

Next Row (WS): Knit to marker, remove marker, knit next stitch with its wrap, k1.

With right side facing you, bind off knitwise to last 2 stitches, k2, leaving 3 stitches on right needle.

MAKE I-CORD

With remaining 3 stitches, work an I-Cord for 3 inches, working last row as follows:

Last Row: K1, k2tog, pass first stitch over second stitch and off right needle. Cut yarn, leaving an 8-inch tail and pull through remaining stitch.

Thread tail onto a tapestry needle. Make a loop with I-cord and weave tail into fabric of washcloth at base of I-cord, then weave it through the looped I-cord, and back into fabric of the washcloth.

Weave in the ends and wet block!

LAYOUT OPTIONS

Here are 5 more ways to play with color. All of these layouts use the above Half + Half Pattern as the foundation, and here's how we did each one….

LAYOUT 1

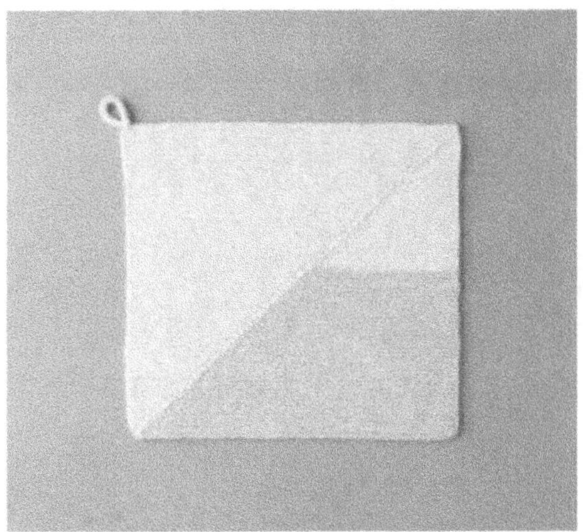

NOTE We knit this layout in two different color schemes: one using Colors E and A and one using Colors D and A. The second version is in parentheses…

Follow the Half + Half Pattern as written, casting on with Color E (D) and using it for 6½ inches of Triangle 1, ending with a wrong-side row. Use Color A for the remainder of Triangle 1, then use Color A for Triangle 2.

LAYOUT 2

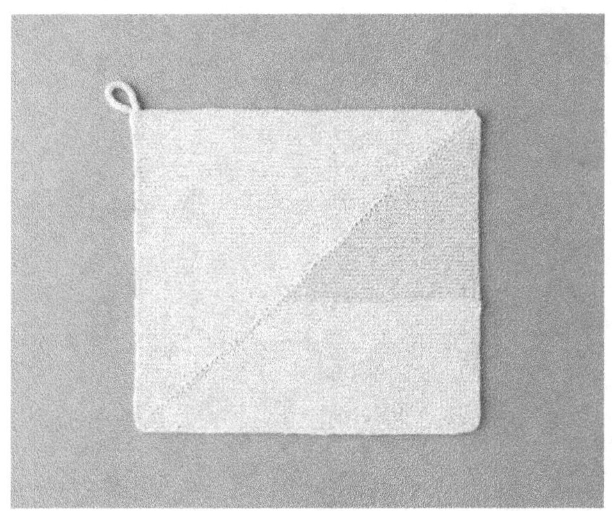

Follow the Half + Half Pattern as written, casting on with Color A and using it for 5 inches of Triangle 1, ending with a wrong-side row. Use Color C for the remainder of Triangle 1, then use Color A for Triangle 2.

LAYOUT 3

NOTE We knit this layout using Colors C, B, and A for one washcloth and Colors D, C, and A for the other. The second version is in parentheses…

Follow the Half + Half Pattern as written, casting on with Color C (D) and using it for 3½ inches of Triangle 1, ending with a wrong-side row. Use Color B (C) for the remainder of Triangle 1, then use Color A for Triangle 2.

LAYOUT 4

Follow the Half + Half Pattern as written, casting on with Color E and using it for 2½ inches of Triangle 1, ending with a wrong-side row. Use Color A for 1½ inches, ending with a wrong-side row, then use Color C for the remainder of Triangle 1. Use Color A for Triangle 2.

LAYOUT 5

Follow the Half + Half Pattern as written, casting on with Color B and using it for 2 inches of Triangle 1, ending with a wrong-side row. Use Color D for 2 inches, ending with a wrong-side row, then use Color C for 2 inches, ending with a wrong-side row, then use Color A for 2 inches, ending with a wrong-side row, then use Color E for the remainder of Triangle 1. Use Color A for Triangle 2.

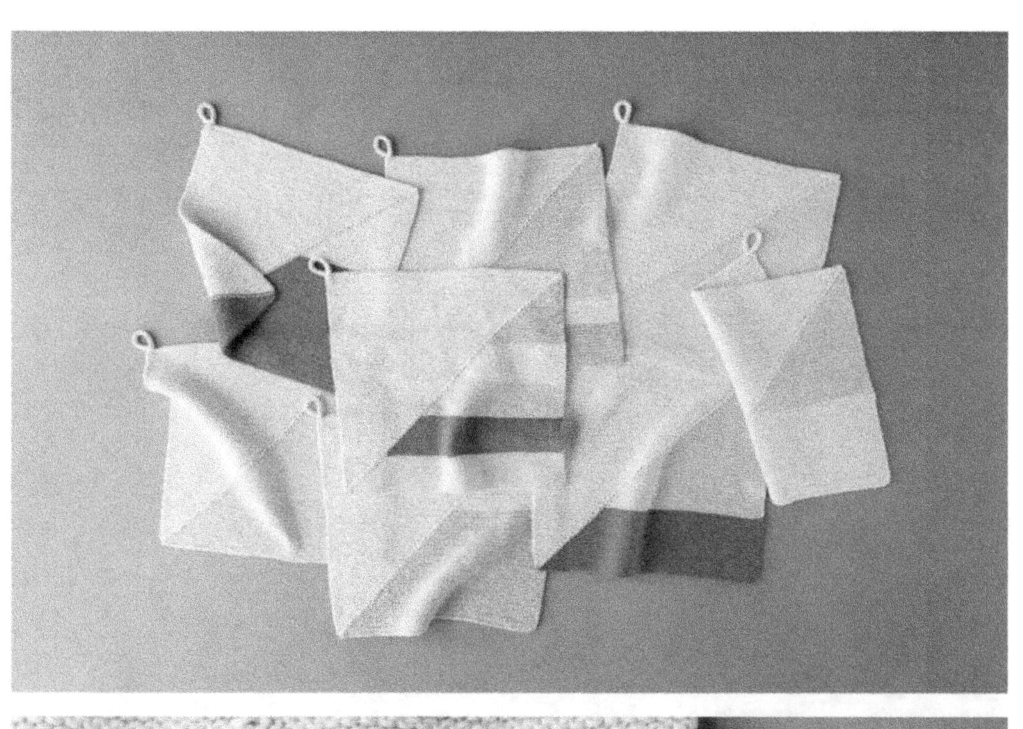